PERFECT LONG-HAIRED CATS

Written by Eliza Jeffery

Illustrated by Marina Halak

Copyright © 2024 Hungry Tomato Ltd

First published in 2024 by Hungry Tomato Ltd
F15, Old Bakery Studios, Blewetts Wharf, Malpas Road, Truro, Cornwall,
TR1 1QH, UK.

No part of this publication may be reproduced, stored in a retrieval system, or transmitted in any form or by any means, electronic, mechanical, photocopying, recording, or otherwise, without prior written permission of the copyright owner.

A CIP catalogue record for this book is available from the British Library.

ISBN 9781835693469

Printed in China

Discover more at
www.hungrytomato.com

CONTENTS

The World of Cats	4
Taking Care of Cats	6
Cool Cat Features	8
Perfect Long-haired Cats	10
Popular Pedigree	11
Iconic Looks	12
Laid-back, Lazy and Loving	14
The Hairiest	16
Great Qualities	18
Special Coats	20
Fur-tastic Cat Facts	22
Tail Talk	24
Name That Cat	26
What's That Cat?	28
Glossary	30
Index	31

Words in **BOLD** can be found in the glossary.

THE WORLD OF CATS

Get ready to explore the wonderful world of cats! From the lovable Persian to the sweet Ragdoll, there are so many different types of amazing cats to discover.

WHAT IS A SPECIES?

A species is a group of living things, like animals or plants, that share **unique** characteristics. For example, cheetahs and **domestic** cats are two different species. There are around 40 cat species in total, some of which can be separated into smaller groups called breeds.

WHAT IS A BREED?

A breed is a small group of animals within a species that all share the same (or very similar) appearance and characteristics, making them easy to identify. There are lots of different breeds, and they can vary wildly in shape, size, hairiness, and personality.

Not all cats belong to a specific breed. Some cats are a mixture of lots of different breeds. They can make fantastic and unique pets, and can often be found looking for a loving home at rescue or **rehoming shelters**.

These cats may have different coats, but they are the same breed!

WHERE DO CATS COME FROM?

All cats are **descendants** of the African wildcat, a species that are believed to have appeared 12 million years ago! This cat is still around today, alongside many other types of wild cat. There are plenty of new species that have been domesticated by humans too – these are the types of cats that we keep as pets!

Some cats like to get up to mischief!

GETTING A CAT?

Maybe you already have a cat in your family, or maybe you'd like to in the future. Owning a cat can be fun and rewarding, but it's also a big responsibility! Some cats need a lot of **grooming**, care, and attention. Before buying or adopting a cat, you should always carefully research their breed and think about whether you are able to give them everything they need to be happy.

TAKING CARE OF CATS

When it comes to taking care of a cat, there is a lot to consider. Some cats need a lot more looking after than others, especially when it comes to grooming! Here are a few things to consider when you are looking into what your cat needs to be happy.

GROOMING

Grooming is a very important part of owning a cat. Cats naturally clean themselves, often spending many hours a day licking their fur clean to stop it **matting** and picking up dirt. Despite doing a lot of the hard work themselves, cats still need some help from their owners!

Some cats require a brush once a week, whereas some require brushing every day! The length of your cat's coat will affect how much attention it requires. Because of this, long-haired cats in particular need a lot of grooming time!

It is recommended that 15-30 minutes per day should be spent grooming your long-haired feline.

Not every cat enjoys grooming, but it is very important for their health. Grooming your cat is a good way to create a strong bond with your cat, as well as check them over for any health problems.

*By helping your cat clean themselves, it lowers the chance of them swallowing large chunks of fur called **fur balls**.*

DIFFERENT COATS

Although most cats have a single coat of fur, some have two coats (double coat), and a handful even have three coats (triple coat)! Make sure you do some research on your cat breed to ensure the best grooming routine.

Some cats, such as the Turkish Angora, have single coats, which gives them silky, smooth, and fine fur.

Cats such as Persians have double coats, which means they have an added extra layer of warmth, and their hair is usually thicker.

Cats like the Siberian have triple coats, which means they have extra layers of fur to help them stay warm in cold weather.

COOL CAT FEATURES

Explore the unique features that make cats such fascinating creatures! From their powerful legs to their clever whiskers, discover the impressive adaptations that help cats thrive in their **environments**.

NOSE

WHISKERS

LEGS

TAIL

WHISKERS

Whiskers are like special tools for cats that help them feel and understand their surroundings. They're as wide as a cat's body and can help them **navigate** in the dark, feel what might be nearby, and even sense vibrations in the air!

TAIL

Cats use their tail to keep their balance and move around easily, thanks to the many muscles found in them. They use their tail to show how they are feeling, too. For example, when a cat's tail is straight up, it means they are happy!

NOSE

Cats have a great sense of smell, which they use for hunting, navigating, and finding familiar scents. Their sense of smell allows them to communicate with other cats, too! They do this by leaving their scent and marking their **territory**.

LEGS

The front legs of a cat are very important for balance, as well as grabbing and holding onto things. The back legs of a cat are very powerful and are used to push a cat forward when they are running or pouncing.

PERFECT LONG-HAIRED CATS

It is believed that domestic cats only began to develop long hair due to **crossbreeding.** These felines have beautiful coats but require a lot of upkeep from their owners!

Long-haired cats often shed their fur, especially during warmer months, and most require grooming every day to keep their coats soft and luxurious. Let's explore the world of lovable long-haired cats!

Longhairs need lots of grooming!

POPULAR PEDIGREE   11

Persian

The Persian cat is extremely popular among cat owners. This glamorous feline is known for its friendly personality, flat face, and thick, silky coat. This is one of the oldest cat breeds, dating all the way back to the 1600s.

Leaves lots of fur everywhere it goes!

Large, round eyes

Thick, feathered tail

ORIGIN: Iran
COAT: Soft and silky
PERSONALITY: Quiet and gentle

GROONING 🐾🐾🐾🐾🐾
AFFECTION 🐾🐾🐾🐾🐾
PLAYFULNESS 🐾🐾🐾

Round head with full, chubby cheeks

12 PERFECT LONG-HAIRED CATS

Birman

This beautiful feline is best known for its bright, blue eyes and thick, soft coat. The Birman loves to be around its owners and can be needy at times, meowing when it would like more attention!

- Piercing, round eyes
- Full cheeks
- White paws like gloves!

ORIGIN: Myanmar (formerly Burma)
COAT: Soft and silky
PERSONALITY: Affectionate and clingy

GROOMING 🐾🐾🐾🐾🐾
AFFECTION 🐾🐾🐾🐾🐾
PLAYFULNESS 🐾🐾🐾🐾🐾

Kurilian Bobtail

The Kurilian bobtail is often described as having a tail similar to a rabbit's! This striking cat has a short but fluffy tail and wild-looking coat. They are very clever, love to play and can be taught tricks.

- Bright, gold/amber eyes
- Large body
- Loves learning new things!

ORIGIN: Kuril Islands
COAT: Soft and silky
PERSONALITY: Sociable and intelligent

GROOMING 🐾🐾🐾🐾🐾
AFFECTION 🐾🐾🐾🐾🐾
PLAYFULNESS 🐾🐾🐾🐾🐾

ICONIC LOOKS   13

Minuet (Napoleon)

Named after the French conqueror Napoleon Bonaparte for its short legs and big personality, this charming cat is a fairly new breed, created by mixing a Munchkin with a Persian (page 11) in the 1990s. The Minuet is sometimes referred to as the "dachshund" of the cat world!

- Long, fluffy tail
- Small ears, set far apart
- Very short, stubby legs

ORIGIN: USA
COAT: Dense and soft
PERSONALITY: Friendly and intelligent

GROOMING 🐾🐾🐾
AFFECTION 🐾🐾🐾🐾🐾
PLAYFULNESS 🐾🐾🐾🐾

Cymric

The Cymric is best known for not having a tail at all! This distinctive feline has an athletic build but doesn't have much energy to play. They do, however, love being around people and are very gentle and loving toward their owners.

- Glossy double coat
- Missing tail
- Prominent whiskers
- Muscular, sturdy legs

ORIGIN: Canada
COAT: Voluminous and thick
PERSONALITY: Well-tempered and sweet

GROOMING 🐾🐾🐾🐾
AFFECTION 🐾🐾🐾🐾
PLAYFULNESS 🐾🐾

14 PERFECT LONG-HAIRED CATS

Ragamuffin

Ragamuffins are a large breed of cat that came from a new development of the Ragdoll (below). These relaxed felines are known for being gentle and patient around children. Although they do enjoy playing, they would much prefer a cuddle!

Large, expressive eyes

Long, thick tail

Large, long and lots of fur!

ORIGIN: USA
COAT: Silky and soft
PERSONALITY: Loyal and laid-back

GROOMING 🐾🐾🐾
AFFECTION 🐾🐾🐾🐾🐾
PLAYFULNESS 🐾🐾🐾

Ragdoll

The Ragdoll is a popular breed among families due to its playfulness, calm nature and friendly expressions. This well-built feline is intelligent and eager to please, spending most of its time following its owners around.

Wide, pointy ears

Bright, blue eyes

Who wouldn't want to give me a cuddle?

Shorter fur on legs

ORIGIN: USA
COAT: Soft and silky
PERSONALITY: Peaceful and sweet

GROOMING 🐾🐾🐾
AFFECTION 🐾🐾🐾🐾🐾
PLAYFULNESS 🐾🐾🐾🐾

LAID-BACK, LAZY AND LOVING   15

British Longhair

British longhair cats have attractive long, flowing coats. These round-faced felines are known for their sweet nature and loyalty to their owners. They are playful as kittens but take on a lazier approach to life as they get older!

Round, golden eyes

Prominent whisker pads

Brush-like tail

ORIGIN: United Kingdom
COAT: Thick and soft
PERSONALITY: Calm and friendly

GROOMING	🐾🐾🐾
AFFECTION	🐾🐾🐾🐾
PLAYFULNESS	🐾🐾

Siberian

The Siberian is an ancient breed from Russia, known for its triple coated fur that helps it stay warm in cold weather. This beautiful feline is very affectionate and enjoys the company of humans, as well as other animals. These large cats take five years to reach full size.

Pink nose

This cat has a very fluffy coat!

Muscular legs

Large, round paws

ORIGIN: Russia
COAT: Water-resistant and soft
PERSONALITY: Friendly and patient

GROOMING	🐾🐾🐾🐾🐾
AFFECTION	🐾🐾🐾🐾🐾
PLAYFULNESS	🐾🐾🐾

PERFECT LONG-HAIRED CATS

Norwegian Forest

Norwegian forest cats are large cats, known for their beautiful silvery fur. Their dense, double coat keeps them warm, becoming even thicker during winter months. These majestic felines love to explore!

Bright green eyes!

White markings on chest

Likes to play outdoors, whatever the weather!

ORIGIN: United Kingdom
COAT: Short and thick
PERSONALITY: Loyal and laid-back

GROOMING 🐾🐾🐾🐾🐾
AFFECTION 🐾🐾🐾🐾🐾
PLAYFULNESS 🐾🐾🐾🐾🐾

Selkirk Rex

With thick, untamed curls, the Selkirk Rex instantly stands out from other breeds. This unusual-coated feline is known for being extremely affectionate, spending most of its time following its owners around. It loves cuddles as much as it loves to play games!

They even have curly whiskers!

Thick, white hair surrounds the neck

Large, round paws

ORIGIN: USA
COAT: Thick and curly
PERSONALITY: Gentle and sociable

GROOMING 🐾🐾🐾🐾🐾
AFFECTION 🐾🐾🐾🐾🐾
PLAYFULNESS 🐾🐾🐾🐾🐾

THE HAIRIEST   17

Somali

You can spot a Somali cat because of its large, fox-like tail. This endearing feline is a long-haired version of the Abyssinian, sharing its striking features and bundles of energy. This cat is known for its impressive jumping and climbing skills!

Almond-shaped eyes

Arched back

Large, bushy tail

ORIGIN: USA

COAT: Fine and soft

PERSONALITY: Energetic and curious

GROOMING	🐾 🐾 🐾 🐾 🐾
AFFECTION	🐾 🐾 🐾 🐾 🐾
PLAYFULNESS	🐾 🐾 🐾 🐾 🐾

LaPerm

Similar to the Selkirk Rex (page 16), the LaPerm has a coat of soft wavy fur and tight curls. They love the company of humans and are known for purring loudly to show they are happy. Charming and sociable, LaPerms are also very active and enjoy playing fetch!

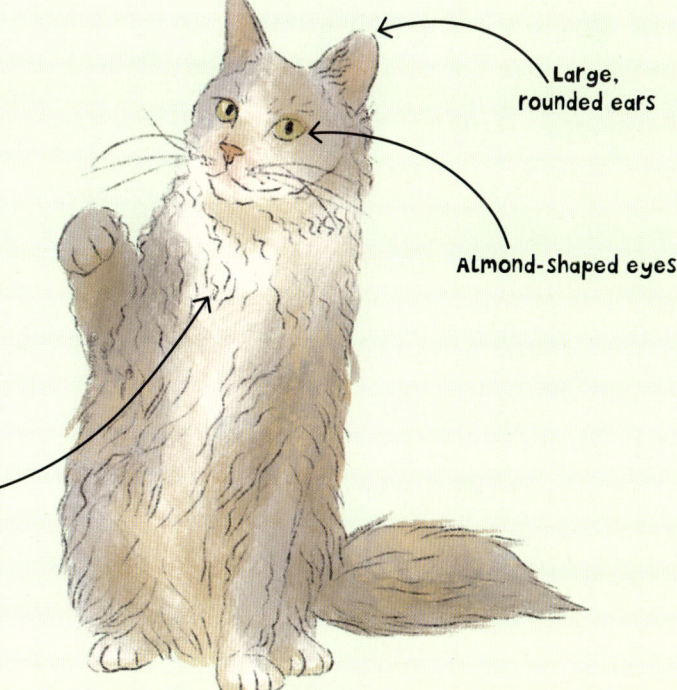

Large, rounded ears

Almond-shaped eyes

Tightest curls around the chest

ORIGIN: USA

COAT: Curly and soft

PERSONALITY: Intelligent and people-loving

GROOMING	🐾 🐾 🐾 🐾 🐾
AFFECTION	🐾 🐾 🐾 🐾 🐾
PLAYFULNESS	🐾 🐾 🐾 🐾 🐾

18 PERFECT LONG-HAIRED CATS

Javanese

Javanese cats are always on the move! Agile and brave, they are often found climbing tall trees, or finding high perches to reach. They are also very vocal cats, happy to let their owners know when they want their food!

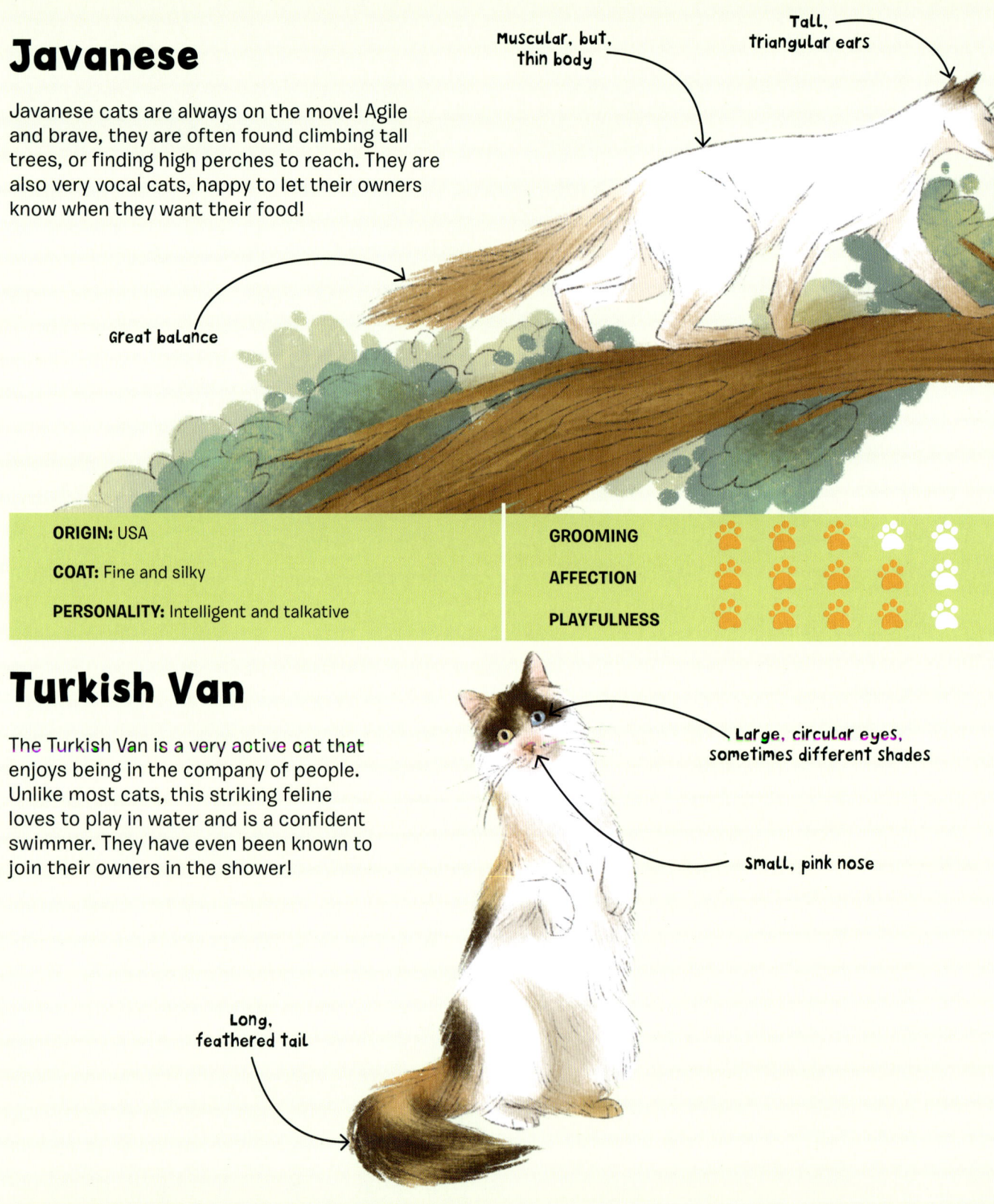

Muscular, but thin body

Tall, triangular ears

Great balance

ORIGIN: USA
COAT: Fine and silky
PERSONALITY: Intelligent and talkative

GROOMING 🐾🐾🐾🐾🐾
AFFECTION 🐾🐾🐾🐾🐾
PLAYFULNESS 🐾🐾🐾🐾🐾

Turkish Van

The Turkish Van is a very active cat that enjoys being in the company of people. Unlike most cats, this striking feline loves to play in water and is a confident swimmer. They have even been known to join their owners in the shower!

Large, circular eyes, sometimes different shades

Small, pink nose

Long, feathered tail

ORIGIN: Turkey
COAT: Fine and soft
PERSONALITY: Energetic and fun-loving

GROOMING 🐾🐾🐾🐾🐾
AFFECTION 🐾🐾🐾🐾🐾
PLAYFULNESS 🐾🐾🐾🐾🐾

GREAT QUALITIES 19

Turkish Angora

This pretty feline is a very rare breed of cat and is considered a national treasure in its origin country of Turkey. They are very sociable, so they don't like to be alone for long periods of time; if they are, Turkish Angoras are known to get up to mischief!

Eyes are often different shades

Long legs for jumping and playing!

Long, bushy tail

ORIGIN: Turkey

COAT: Glossy and soft

PERSONALITY: Intelligent and friendly

GROOMING 🐾🐾🐾
AFFECTION 🐾🐾🐾🐾🐾
PLAYFULNESS 🐾🐾🐾🐾

PERFECT LONG-HAIRED CATS

Himalayan

Himalayan cats are a mix of the popular breeds, Persian (page 11) and Siamese, and originated in the early 1900s. This large feline is known for its extremely thick coat and bright, blue eyes. This cat loves a snooze!

Small, pointy ears

Large, round paws

Needs lots of grooming

ORIGIN: USA
COAT: Dense and silky
PERSONALITY: Sweet and gentle

GROOMING
AFFECTION
PLAYFULNESS

York Chocolate

York chocolate cats are known for their luxuriously soft coats. They are affectionate pets and love to be surrounded by people. As much as these pretty felines love a cuddle on their owner's lap, they are also skilled hunters outdoors too.

Thick, bushy tail

Thin neck

Strong, sturdy legs

ORIGIN: USA
COAT: Thick and soft
PERSONALITY: Curious and loving

GROOMING
AFFECTION
PLAYFULNESS

SPECIAL COATS 21

Nebelung

The Nebelung has a really thick coat, specifically the mane-like fur that surrounds its neck. This handsome breed prefers a quiet environment over a busy household and is often found sleeping on the lap of its owner!

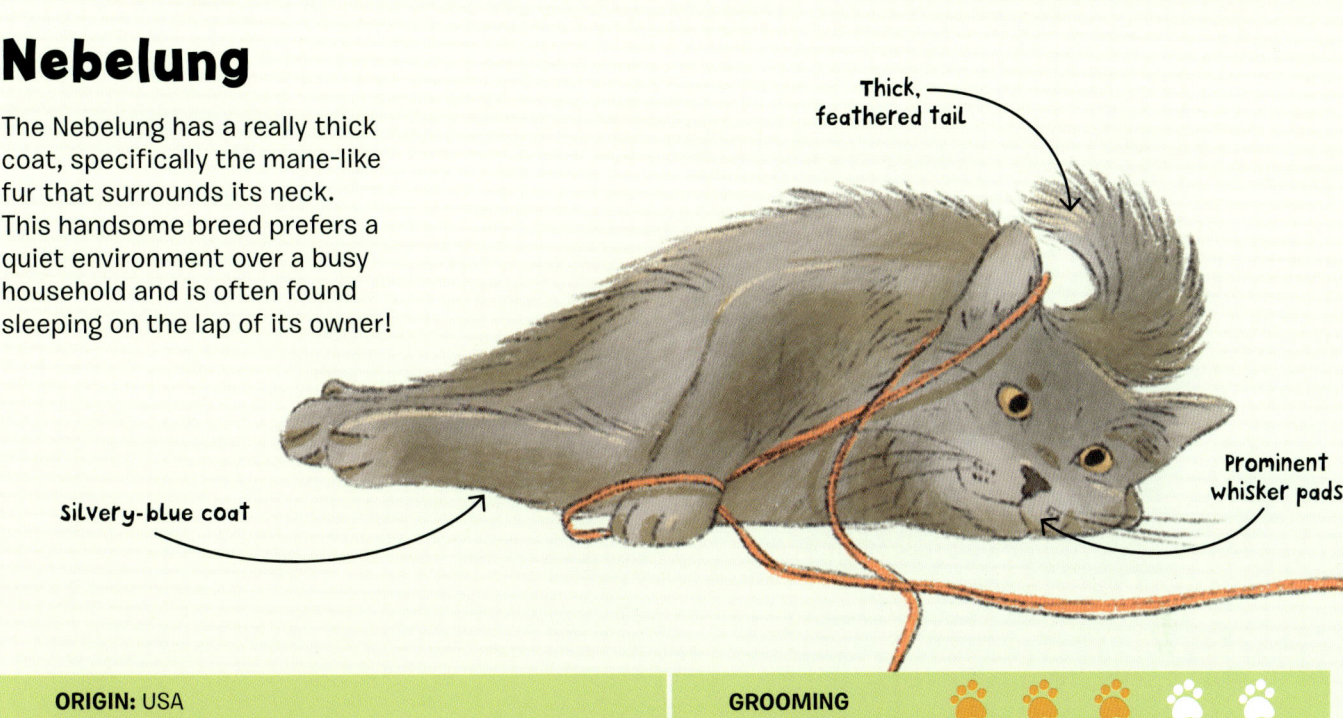

Thick, feathered tail

Prominent whisker pads

Silvery-blue coat

ORIGIN: USA
COAT: Dense and heavy
PERSONALITY: Loyal and shy

GROOMING
AFFECTION
PLAYFULNESS

Balinese

The Balinese is the long-haired variant of the Siamese, sharing many of its striking features. They have beautiful flowing coats and dark blue eyes that make them a well-known breed. These beautiful felines live for attention and often demand it from their owners by meowing!

Darker markings around its face, ears and tail!

Large, rounded ears

Long, thin body

ORIGIN: USA
COAT: Silky and close to the body
PERSONALITY: Outgoing and curious

GROOMING
AFFECTION
PLAYFULNESS

FUR-TASTIC CAT FACTS

What else is there to know about the amazing world of long-haired cats? Let's uncover more intriguing facts about these fluffy felines.

UNIQUE NOSE

Every cat's nose print is unique, just like human fingerprints are! Every feline has a different pattern of ridges, bumps, and lines on their nose. These individual patterns can help to tell our feline friends apart!

WISE WHISKERS

Not only do whiskers help cats navigate their way in the dark, they can also show how a cat is feeling! When a cat's whiskers are firmly pulled around their face, it suggests they might be feeling **threatened**, while relaxed whiskers mean your cat is feeling happy and relaxed.

This cat is feeling happy and relaxed.

GINGER GENE

Around 80% of all ginger cats in the world are male! So if you see a ginger cat, it's more than likely that it is a boy. Because of this, female ginger cats are very rare!

SLEEPY FELINES

Cats are known for their naps. On average, a cat will sleep between 13-16 hours a day! As these sleepy felines get older, they will sometimes sleep for even longer. Kittens need lots of rest, too!

Some breeds are a lot lazier than others, so they sleep more often!

TAIL TALK

Unlike dogs, cats are very hard to read! So, it's important to know the different ways that cats communicate how they feel. One of those ways is through their tails!

Annoyed or impatient
Flicking their tail from side to side is a sign that your cat is annoyed or being impatient.

Happy
Tail pointing straight up to the sky is a sign that your cat is very happy and wants some attention!

Ready to pounce
Tail curved over their back, towards their head is a sign that your cat is getting ready to pounce!

Happy and excited
Tail pointing straight up and shaking is a sign that your cat is so happy that they are shaking with excitement!

Frustrated or excited
Hitting their tail against the floor is a sign that your cat is either frustrated or excited.

Obedient or worried
Tail tucked between their legs and arched back is a sign that your cat is being **obedient** or that they are worried.

Threatened
Tail fluffed out is a sign that your cat is feeling threatened.

Calm and relaxed
Tail out straight, or slightly low to the floor is a sign that your cat is feeling calm and relaxed.

Based on the information to the left, can you work out how each cat in these images is feeling? Use the options below each image to help you out.

1

Threatened | Frustrated or excited

2

Calm and relaxed | Ready to pounce

3

Calm and relaxed | Happy

4

Obedient or worried | Threatened

Answers can be found on page 32.

NAME THAT CAT

Can you work out which cat each of these pictures are a part of? Clues have been provided for you based on facts in this book.

CLUE: These cats have soft, wavy fur and tight curls.

CLUE: These cats are often found climbing trees.

CLUE: These cats are recognisable for their large, fox-like tail.

CLUE: These cats have triple coated fur, and take five years to reach full size.

CLUE: These cats have tails similar to rabbits.

CLUE: These cats are considered a national treasure in their home country.

CLUE: These cats love to play in water and are confident swimmers.

CLUE: These cats have short, stubby legs and a big personality.

CLUE: These cats are long-haired variants of the Siamese cat.

CLUE: These cats are one of the oldest cat breeds and are extremely popular.

Answers can be found on page 32.

WHAT'S THAT CAT?

Now that you have read all about these long-haired cats, how good are you at identifying them? There are 20 different cats to figure out. Use the information in the book to help you.

What am I?
A. Kurilian Bobtail
B. Siberian
C. Turkish Van

What am I?
A. Selkirk rex
B. Turkish Angora
C. Javanese

What am I?
A. Nebelung
B. Somali
C. Turkish Angora

What am I?
A. Ragdoll
B. Norwegian Forest
C. British Longhair

What am I?
A. Balinese
B. Norwegian Forest
C. Selkirk Rex

What am I?
A. Birman
B. Minuet (Napoleon)
C. Himalayan

What am I?
A. LaPerm
B. Minuet (Napoleon)
C. Persian

What am I?
A. Ragauffin
B. Himalayan
C. Balinese

What am I?
A. York Chocolate
B. Somali
C. Siberian

What am I?
A. Turkish Van
B. Birman
C. Turkish Angora

Answers can be found on page 32.

What am I?
A. Nebelung
B. British Longhair
C. Ragamuffin

What am I?
A. Somali
B. Himalayan
C. Siberian

What am I?
A. Turkish Van
B. Nebelung
C. Cymric

What am I?
A. Cymric
B. Selkrik Rex
C. York Chocolate

What am I?
A. LaPerm
B. Ragdoll
C. Kurilian Bobtail

What am I?
A. Ragdoll
B. Persian
C. Javanese

What am I?
A. Birman
B. York Chocolate
C. Balinese

What am I?
A. Persian
B. LaPerm
C. Selkrik Rex

What am I?
A. Javanese
B. Cymric
C. Kurilian Bobtail

What am I?
A. British Longhair
B. Norwegian Forest
C. Ragamuffin

GLOSSARY

Crossbreeding - when two cats of different breeds have kittens.

Descendants - people or animals that are related to an individual or group who lived in the past. For example, you are a descendant of your parents and grandparents.

Domestic - an animal that has been tamed or trained to live or work with humans.

Environments - another word for surroundings.

Fur balls - clumps of fur that animals sometimes cough up, usually from grooming (see below).

Grooming - when animals clean themselves, often by licking their fur or feathers.

Matting - when an animal's fur gets tangled and stuck together. This is usually because it hasn't been brushed or groomed.

Navigate - to plan and follow a route, in order to get somewhere.

Obedient - when someone or something listens and follows instructions, like a dog that sits when it is told to.

Rehoming shelter - a place where cats (or other animals) who were lost, stray or given up by their owners are looked after until they can be adopted into a new home.

Territory - a specific area that belongs to someone or something.

Threatened - being in danger or at risk of harm.

Unique - something that stands out and is completely different from everything else.

INDEX

B
Balinese 21, 28-29, 32
Birman 12, 28-29, 32
British longhair 15, 28-29, 32

C
crossbreed 10, 30
Cymric 13, 28-29, 32

F
features 8-9, 17, 21
    legs 8-9, 13, 14-15, 19, 20, 24, 27
    nose 8-9, 15, 18, 22
    tail 8-9, 11, 12-13, 14-15, 17, 20-21, 24-25, 26, 32
    whiskers 8-9, 13, 16, 22

G
grooming 5, 6-7, 10, 20, 30

H
Himalayan 20, 28-29, 32

J
Javanese 18, 28-29, 32

K
Kurilian bobtail 12, 28-29, 32

L
LaPerm 17, 28-29, 32

M
Minuet (Napoleon) 13, 28-29, 32

N
Nebelung 21, 28-29, 32
Norwegian Forest 16, 28-29, 32

P
Persian 4, 7, 11, 13, 20, 28-29, 32

R
Ragamuffin 14, 28-29, 32
Ragdoll 4, 14, 28-29, 32

S
Selkirk rex 16-17, 28, 32
Siberian 7, 15, 28-29, 32
Somali 17, 28-29, 32
species 4-5

T
Turkish angora 7, 19, 28-29, 32
Turkish van 18, 28-29, 32

Y
York chocolate 20, 28-29, 32

TAIL TALK ANSWERS

1 - Threatened
2 - Ready to pounce
3 - Calm and relaxed
4 - Obedient or worried

NAME THAT CAT ANSWERS

1 - LaPerm
2 - Javanese
3 - Somali
4 - Siberian
5 - Kurilian Bobtail
6 - Turkish Van
7 - Turkish Angora
8 - Minuet (Napoleon)
9 - Balinese
10 - Persian

WHAT'S THAT CAT ANSWERS

1 - A. Kurilian Bobtail
2 - A. Selkirk Rex
3 - C. Turkish Angora
4 - C. British Longhair
5 - B. Norwegian Forest
6 - A. Birman
7 - B. Minuet (Napoleon)
8 - B. Himalayan
9 - C. Siberian
10 - A. Turkish Van
11 - A. Nebelung
12 - A. Somali
13 - C. Cymric
14 - C. York Chocolate
15 - B. Ragdoll
16 - B. Persian
17 - C. Balinese
18 - B. LaPerm
19 - A. Javanese
20 - C. Ragamuffin

Picture Credits:
(abbreviations: t=top, b=bottom, m=middle, l=left, r=right)

Shutterstock: Allison McAdams 29tl; Andreas Krumwiede 23bl; Babkina Svetlana 24 (all cat silhouettes); Bachkova Natalia 9bl; Borkin Vadim 28ml; CHUANGXIN ZHOU 28tr; Ciprian Gherghias 29tr; Compass Crew 9br; Daria Gorbunova 25tl; Ecuadorplanet 28mr; Elisa Putti 9tr, 28ml; Ground Picture 23tr; Jilin Su 28tl; Just-Mila 28bl; Linn Currie 29ml; Lithian 25tr; Massimo Cattaneo 25ml; Monika Wroblewska 29bl; Murr Photo 22tl; Nataliya Kuznetsova 29tl; Nynke Van Holten 28br; OrangeGroup 28tl; Pernilla Westh 29tr; Regina Hoenes 9tl; Robert Way 28mr; Scampi 29br; Sergio Photone 22br; Svyatoslav Balan 28tr; Yhelfman 25mr.

Every effort has been made to trace the copyright holders, and we apologise in advance for any unintentional omissions. We would be pleased to insert the appropriate acknowledgements in any subsequent edition of this publication.

ABOUT THE AUTHOR

Eliza Jeffery is a children's book author based in Falmouth. She is passionate about helping children explore and enjoy the big world around them. She loves exploring Cornwall, and can often be found reading a book and eating a bowl of mussels by the sea!

ABOUT THE ILLUSTRATOR

Marina Halak is a talented illustrator of children's books from Ukraine. Her stunning illustrations are inspired by her own childhood, children, nature, magical moments and fairy tales. Marina is also the illustrator behind the series, *Dogs*.